Madam
C. J. Walker

Self-made millionaire Madam C. J. Walker used this portrait of herself in advertisements for her popular hair-care products.

JUNIOR ▪ WORLD ▪ BIOGRAPHIES

A JUNIOR *BLACK AMERICANS OF ACHIEVEMENT* BOOK

Madam C. J. Walker

Marian W. Taylor

CHELSEA JUNIORS

a division of CHELSEA HOUSE PUBLISHERS

Chelsea House Publishers

EDITORIAL DIRECTOR Richard Rennert
EXECUTIVE MANAGING EDITOR Karyn Gullen Browne
EXECUTIVE EDITOR Sean Dolan
COPY CHIEF Robin James
PICTURE EDITOR Adrian G. Allen
ART DIRECTOR Robert Mitchell
MANUFACTURING DIRECTOR Gerald Levine
PRODUCTION COORDINATOR Marie Claire Cebrián-Ume

JUNIOR WORLD BIOGRAPHIES

SENIOR EDITOR Kathy Kuhtz

Staff for MADAM C. J. WALKER

COPY EDITOR Nicole Greenblatt
EDITORIAL ASSISTANT Kelsey Goss
PICTURE RESEARCHER Sandy Jones
SERIES DESIGN Marjorie Zaum
DESIGNER John Infantino
COVER ILLUSTRATION Janet Hamlin, from a photograph of Madam C. J.
Walker from the Walker Collection of A'Lelia Bundles.

First Printing

1 3 5 7 9 8 6 4 2

Library of Congress Cataloging-in-Publication Data
Taylor, Marian W.
    Madam C. J. Walker / Marian W. Taylor
      p. cm.—(Junior world biographies)
    Includes bibliographical references and index.
Summary: Presents the life of the black laundress who founded a cosmetics
company and became the first female self-made millionaire in the United
States.
ISBN 0-7910-2039-8
    0-7910-2040-1 (pbk.)
1. Walker, C. J., Madam, 1867–1919—Juvenile literature. 2. Afro-
American women executives—Biography—Juvenile literature. 3. Women
millionaires—United States— Biography—Juvenile literature. 4. Cosmetics
industry—United States—History—Juvenile literature. [1. Walker, C. J.,
Madam, 1867–1919. 2. Businesswomen. 3. Afro-Americans—Biography.]
I. Title. II. Series.
HD9970.5.C672W358 1993   93-14653
338.7'66855'092—dc20   CIP
[B]   AC

Contents

Madam C. J. Walker poses for a photograph in 1910, two years before the National Negro Business League (NNBL) meeting in Chicago, Illinois. By this time, she was selling her Walker System of hair care all over the nation.

1

"A Remarkable Woman"

Sarah Breedlove Walker arrived in Chicago, Illinois, in 1912. She was a tall, self-confident businesswoman, 44 years old. Walker was chief of her own company, which made hair products for black women. She had come to Chicago to meet with 200 other members of the National Negro Business League (NNBL).

The NNBL's president was 56-year-old Booker T. Washington. He was head of Tuskegee Institute, America's most important college for blacks. (At this time, whites and blacks almost never went to the same schools or colleges.) Washington was probably the best-known black person in America. He was admired by citizens of all races. Many people asked his advice about racial matters, even presidents of the United States.

Walker suspected that Washington looked down on her work. She also suspected that he did not believe in women's rights. Still, he had treated her politely when she visited Tuskegee. He said he appreciated her work to raise money for black colleges. She was sure he would allow her to speak at one of the NNBL sessions.

When the NNBL members got together, they told each other about their work. Some had made huge amounts of money selling houses. Others had gotten rich by opening stores or factories. What made these success stories truly special was the race of the speakers: all were black. All had come a long way.

Less than 50 years earlier, almost all the blacks in America had been *slaves*. One out of every seven Americans, in fact, was owned by another person. Many NNBL members, including Booker T. Washington, had been born into slavery. Others were the children of slaves.

American slavery ended in 1865. At that time, a small number of newly freed blacks opened businesses. Most of them were barbershops, food-serving firms, sail-making shops, funeral homes, and drugstores. By 1912, about 40,000 U.S. blacks had their own businesses. But black businessmen were still rare, and black businesswomen were even rarer.

Madam Walker had been poor for most of her life. Then, at the age of 37, she invented a new hair-care product. Seven years later, she owned her own thriving business. It was called the Madam C. J. Walker Manufacturing Company, and it was located in Indianapolis, Indiana. Walker was eager to talk about her life. She was sure it would encourage other black women.

At one of the NNBL sessions in Chicago, an important black newspaper publisher stood up. "I arise to ask this convention for a few minutes of its time to hear a remarkable woman," he said. "She is Madam Walker, the manufacturer of hair goods and preparations."

Washington, who was chairman of the meeting, pretended that he did not hear the publisher. Although other women had addressed the meeting, he did not want Walker to talk before the group. But Walker refused to let this discourage her. She wanted to speak, and she *would* speak. Patiently, she listened to one man after another all day. At the next morning's meeting, she made her move.

"Surely you are not going to shut the door in my face," she said firmly. "I feel that I am in a business that is a credit to the womanhood of our race. I started in business seven years ago with only $1.50." The audience looked at her with curiosity. Who *was* this large, handsome speaker with beautifully groomed hair?

"I am a woman who came from the cotton fields of the South," declared Walker. "I was promoted from there to the washtub." Walker expected people to laugh at this, and they did. Imagine being "promoted" to the job of washerwoman! "Then I was promoted to the cook kitchen, and from there *I promoted myself* into the business of manufacturing hair goods and preparations," Walker continued in a strong voice. "I have built my own factory on my own ground."

Now the audience stopped laughing and started to pay attention. "My object in life is not simply to make money for myself or to spend it on myself," Walker said. "I love to use a part of what I make in trying to help others." When she finished her speech, a storm of applause filled the meeting room.

That evening, NNBL members crowded around Walker to ask questions. Walker said she believed that more black women should strike out on their own. "The girls and women of our race," she said, "must not be afraid to take hold of business endeavor and . . . wring success out of a number of business opportunities that lie at their very doors."

Walker told the NNBL members how her program helped black women. First, a woman studied at a Walker school or took a mail-order course. When she had learned the Walker System of hair care, she became a Walker agent. Then she could work out of her own home. Walker said that

her agents found new freedom and made more money. This allowed them to buy houses and send their children to school.

By the time she went to the Chicago meeting, Walker had trained more than 1,000 women. In 1912, the average black woman worker made $1.50 per week. Walker said her agents were making $5, $10, and even $15 *per day.* "I have

Friends of Indianapolis's new black YMCA gather on its steps in 1913. Walker (first row, second from left) stands next to civil rights leader Booker T. Washington (third from left). Standing in the back row are Freeman Briley Ransom (left), Walker's lawyer, and Colonel Joseph Ward, her doctor.

13

made it possible," she said proudly, "for many colored women to abandon the washtub for more pleasant and profitable occupation."

Several months after the Chicago meeting, Booker T. Washington went to Indianapolis, Indiana, for the opening of a new black YMCA building. Walker was one of the speakers at the opening ceremony. Washington learned that she had given $1,000 to the YMCA building fund, a huge sum in 1912.

At the ceremony, Washington addressed the 1,200 guests. He said that the new YMCA would improve the lives of the city's young men. He also praised Walker for her generous gift, and—to her pleasant surprise—for her work. He said she had started "a business we should all be proud of."

The next NNBL meeting was held a year later. This time, Washington called Walker to the stage. He said, "I now take pleasure in introducing to the convention one of the most progressive and successful businesswomen of our race—Madam C. J. Walker."

When Walker finished her speech, Washington praised her for "all she has done for our race." Then he added some words she must have loved to hear. "You talk about what the men are doing in a business way," he said. "Why, if we don't watch out, the women will excel us!"

That was exactly what Walker intended to do.

A sharecroppers' child helps her father pick cotton.
Walker probably started carrying water to other
field-workers when she was five.

2

Hardships
and Hopes

Madam C. J. Walker was born Sarah Breedlove on December 23, 1867. She lived on a cotton plantation in Delta, Louisiana. Her parents, Owen and Minerva Breedlove, had started their lives as slaves. Sarah was the first member of her family to be born free.

The year Sarah was born was a hard one for Owen and Minerva Breedlove. The 1867 cotton crop had been spoiled by *bollworms* just before harvesttime. When Christmas arrived, the Breedloves had no money to buy presents for Sarah's brother and sister, Alex and Louvenia. Sarah was the family's special and only gift.

The Civil War had ended in 1865, two years before Sarah's birth. The South's slaves became free, but many did not know what to do next. Some left the plantations, but even more stayed on as *sharecroppers*. Owen and Minerva Breedlove were among this group.

The man who had once owned the Breedloves gave them the use of land, seed, and tools. In return, they gave him a share of the crops they raised. They worked very hard, but they could not get ahead. At the end of each growing season, they owed the landowner more than they had earned. The owners always got the most out of the sharecropper system. Most of the "croppers" were just as poor as they had been when they were slaves.

Minerva Breedlove could not afford even one day without working. She chopped cotton right up to the day of Sarah's birth. She had the baby in the one-room, unpainted shack she shared with her family. Its roof leaked, and the windows had no glass. Wind from the nearby Mississippi River whistled through the wooden shutters.

The Breedloves wanted their children to have more than this. They had never learned to read or write, but they knew *literacy* was a sign of freedom. They dreamed of sending Sarah and her siblings to school.

But this was the post–Civil War South. It was not easy for any poor people to get an education. For black people, it was almost impossible. Many southerners believed that blacks had no business in school. Some joined *racist* bands such as the Ku Klux Klan and the White Brotherhood.

These hate-filled bands spent most of their time scaring and abusing black people. They often burned down black schoolhouses. Sometimes they even killed black teachers and their pupils.

Another circumstance that kept Sarah and her siblings out of school was work. Sarah started working in the fields when she was about five years

Walker was born Sarah Breedlove in this one-room cabin in Delta, Louisiana, on December 23, 1867. Her family was very poor, and she was their only Christmas present.

old. She carried water to the older workers and soon went on to planting. She dropped seeds into the long furrows made by the men and women who pushed the plows.

Every morning, Sarah, Louvenia, and their mother got up at sunrise. First, they cooked breakfast. They always had the same food: corn bread and fried salt pork. After that, they started dinner. This was a meal of vegetables, boiled all day in an iron pot. Sarah watched her mother and older sister carefully.

She learned quickly. In the evenings, she dug potatoes from the garden, swept the yard, and fed the chickens. She also collected the chickens' eggs. The family sold them to make a few extra pennies.

Saturdays were for laundry. From sunrise until dark, Sarah, Louvenia, and Minerva washed clothes in big wooden tubs on the riverbank. They did laundry for themselves and for white people, who paid them about one dollar per week. Washing clothes was as hard as picking cotton. The white people's sheets and tablecloths were huge. When they were soaking wet, they were very heavy, especially for a little girl.

But Sarah did not complain. She loved to listen to her mother and the other women sing while they did the wash. Sometimes their voices blended with the steamboat whistles from the river. Then Sarah would imagine herself traveling. She thought about going to Vicksburg, the Mississippi town across the river—or even farther. But most of the time, she just worked hard.

From time to time, disease broke out in the river towns. It spread quickly in the hot, humid climate. In 1874, when Sarah was seven years old, a severe outbreak of *yellow fever* killed many people in Delta. Two of the victims were Owen and Minerva Breedlove.

Sarah missed her parents terribly. But no one seemed to have time to worry about one lonesome, frightened little girl. The Breedlove children tried to farm, but they could not manage alone. Finally, Sarah's brother Alex moved to Vicksburg to look for work.

Now Sarah and Louvenia were alone on the farm. They found life harder than ever. Sarah longed to go to school, but she and her sister spent almost all their time at their washtubs. They were trying to make enough money to stay alive.

Sometimes Sarah had a few minutes to herself at the end of the day. When she could, she used this precious time to sit on the riverbank. She looked across at Vicksburg and day-dreamed. She liked to watch the ferryboats landing. She would look with wide eyes at the women travelers in their beautiful clothes. Their gowns were very different from her own patched and faded dress.

In 1878, the cotton crop failed again. Thousands of blacks, including the Breedloves, lost their homes. The girls decided to move across the river, where Louvenia got a job as a washerwoman. She was lucky. In Vicksburg, very few black people found work.

One day in 1879, 11-year-old Sarah stood on a Vicksburg dock. She waved as a northbound steamboat puffed up the river. She wished she were aboard, heading for a new life. Instead, she was living in a drafty shack with her sister and new brother-in-law. Louvenia's husband treated Sarah unkindly. She was afraid of him and his bad temper.

Three years later, Sarah escaped from her brother-in-law. At the age of 14, she married Moses McWilliams, a Vicksburg laborer. She did it, she said, "to get a home of my own." Moses worked odd jobs, repairing streets and picking cotton. Sarah kept on working as a washerwoman, as she had since she was a little girl back in Delta.

On June 6, 1885, 17-year-old Sarah gave birth to a daughter. She and her husband named their little girl Lelia. Now Sarah was busier than ever, but she was content. She would work very hard, and someday she would make Lelia's life easier than her own. Soon after Lelia's second birthday, however, Moses McWilliams was killed in an accident.

At 19, Sarah was suddenly a widow and a single mother. She wondered how she could manage on her own. Then her neighbors told her that there were jobs for laundresses in St. Louis.

They said wages there were higher than those in Vicksburg.

All her life, Sarah had listened to train whistles echoing through the night. With hungry eyes, she had watched steamboats sail away to new and exciting places. It was time, she decided, to move on. With a baby on her hip and a boat ticket in her hand, she boarded a northbound riverboat. No matter what the future brought, she told herself, it had to be better than the past.

A *washerwoman scrubs clothes in wooden tubs. Walker spent much of her early life washing laundry to support herself and her daughter, Lelia.*

3

The Road
to Fame

Sarah McWilliams watched her daughter skip off to school and smiled. She was now giving Lelia what she lacked herself—an education. That made all her sacrifices seem worthwhile.

McWilliams walked through her St. Louis rooming house to the backyard. There, on the rickety porch, stood her wooden washtubs. Years later, she remembered the moment: "As I bent over the washboard and looked at my arms buried in the soapsuds, I said to myself, 'What are you going

to do when you grow old and your back gets stiff?'
This set me to thinking, but with all my thinking,
I couldn't see how I, a poor washerwoman, was
going to better my condition."

McWilliams looked at the baskets piled
with dirty clothes. Then she sighed and wiped her
hands on her long apron. She mopped the sweat
from her forehead with her sleeve. Life was hard.
But she knew hers was better than it had been
when she left Vicksburg six years ago.

Being a washerwoman was endless work.
Still, it was better than the only other choice—
being a live-in servant. Washing clothes at home
meant she could keep an eye on Lelia.

McWilliams took pride in her work. She
carefully scrubbed and starched and neatly ironed
her customers' clothes. When she delivered them,
she carried them in a basket balanced on her head.
Her delivery route often led her over a great bridge
that spanned the Mississippi River. She wanted to
build a bridge herself—one that would lead to a

This is the Mississippi River bridge that Walker used to cross when she was a washerwoman in St. Louis. It inspired her to try and build a bridge to a better life.

good life for herself and Lelia. In her prayers, she asked God to show her the way to do it.

McWilliams believed God would help her, but she also believed in helping herself. She worked long hours and spent little of her wages. Each week, she managed to put aside a little money. When Lelia graduated from high school, her proud mother could afford to send her to college in Knoxville, Tennessee.

Soon after McWilliams moved to St. Louis, she had joined an African Methodist Episcopal

church. The women of the church had been friend-
ly and generous to her. She was very grateful and
vowed that someday she, too, would help others
in need.

Several of these church women were well
educated and wealthy. McWilliams was dazzled
by their stylish clothes and formal manners. She
was also impressed because they were community
leaders. She looked at these self-confident, well-
groomed women and then thought about how she
looked herself.

McWilliams thought if she looked better,
she might be as confident as these women. She
always wore neat, crisply starched clothing, but
she was embarrassed about her hair. It was broken
and patchy, and her scalp showed through in some
places.

Many black women had McWilliams's hair
problems. Sometimes hair loss was caused by poor
nutrition and bad health. Sometimes it came from
using lotions made with harmful chemicals. Black
newspapers were full of advertisements for hair-

improvement products. McWilliams tried several hair mixtures, but they did not help.

For a few months, she worked as a sales agent for a hair-lotion company. When she was not washing clothes, she sold hair creams from door to door. Then she got a better idea: if she could make a hair grower and scalp treatment that really worked, she could go into business for herself.

In early 1905, McWilliams told her friends that she had learned how to make the mixture she wanted. She said, "God answered my prayer, for one night I had a dream, and in that dream a big black man appeared to me and told me what to mix up for my hair. . . . I mixed it, put it on my scalp, and in a few weeks my hair was coming in faster than it had ever fallen out. . . . I made up my mind I would begin to sell it."

McWilliams decided to go West to start her new business. She was excited, but she would miss her good friend, Charles Joseph ("C. J.") Walker. He was a well-educated man who worked for a local black newspaper. Promising to write to him, she headed West.

At the age of 37, McWilliams left the Mississippi River area for the first time. On July 21, 1905, she arrived in Denver, Colorado. In her purse she had her life's savings: $1.50. This was one week's pay for her work as a laundress.

McWilliams rented a room, joined a church, and got a job as a cook. She worked all day and stirred up hair products all evening. She tested them on herself and her neighbors. At last, she came up with three mixtures that satisfied her. She called them Wonderful Hair Grower, Glossine, and Vegetable Shampoo.

As usual, McWilliams had been saving her money. Soon, she was able to quit her cook's job. To make money for food and rent, she took in laundry two days a week. She spent the rest of her time going from one house to the next, showing her new products.

McWilliams was a good saleswoman. To get women interested in her hair mixtures, she gave free treatments. First, she washed a customer's hair with Vegetable Shampoo. Then she applied her Wonderful Hair Grower. To complete the treatment, she put a little Glossine on the hair and pressed it with a heated metal comb. This softened the tight curls that people of African descent often have.

Denver's black women liked McWilliams's wares, and they bought more and more of them. She used her profits to buy advertising in the local black newspaper. People soon began buying the hair products by mail order.

But McWilliams was her own best advertisement. She would show customers a "before" picture of herself, when she had patchy, broken hair. Then she would point to her current crop of long, shiny hair—the result, she said, of using her own products. At this point, her customers would usually place large orders.

McWilliams wrote to her St. Louis friend C. J. Walker about her growing business. After a while, he came to visit her in Denver. Not long after that, he asked her to marry him. She said yes. Their wedding took place on January 4, 1906.

Walker helped his wife expand her mail-order business. Together, they manufactured and sold several new products, including Madam C. J. Walker's Wonderful Hair Grower. After her marriage, Sarah Walker began calling herself Madam. She thought it would give her products more appeal.

The Walkers' business was soon bringing in $10 per week. C. J. said the company had gone as far as it could go. But Sarah did not think so. She was sure that many more women would buy her Wonderful Hair Grower if they knew about it. She decided to make a long sales trip.

Her husband laughed at her. He said she would not even earn enough to pay her expenses. She left anyway. In September 1906, she started her trip. It would last a year and a half and cover nine states. Among them were Oklahoma, Louisiana, Mississippi, and New York.

Within a few months, Walker was making weekly sales of $35. That was more than twice as much as the average white American male worker made. It was 10 times the salary of the average black female worker.

By this time, Lelia had graduated from college. She came to Denver to help run the mail-

Walker's daughter, Lelia, holds a rose in this 1907 portrait. After finishing college, Lelia moved to Denver to help run her mother's business. She also posed as a model in several advertisements for Walker's products.

order business while her mother traveled. Lelia was almost six feet tall and stood very straight. Some people thought she looked like a queen and said she gave the company added glamour. She also gave the company extra talent. She turned out to be good at business. Helping to fill the orders her mother kept sending in, she worked hard.

On the road, Sarah Walker was doing more than selling. She was also training agents to demonstrate her products. Women knew they would get part of the profits from whatever they sold. By spring 1908, Walker's company had dozens of representatives and a monthly income of $400. Walker now decided to move East, where more black people lived.

She picked Pittsburgh, Pennsylvania, as her new base. In the summer of 1908, she and Lelia opened a beauty parlor there. They also started Lelia College, a training school for Walker agents. As soon as it opened, it filled up with students. Over the next two years, the college turned out dozens of "hair culturists." In 1910, the *Pennsyl-*

vania Negro Business Directory ran a feature story about Walker. The magazine called her "one of the most successful businesswomen of the race in this community."

As Walker became more and more famous, Pittsburgh's most important black citizens began to notice her. Now, clergymen and women who headed community organizations invited her to their parties and meetings. The kind of people Walker had once admired from afar were now admiring *her*.

Walker drives her battery-powered electric car. She loved automobiles and always bought herself and her daughter the latest models.

4

"The Money Making Wonder"

In 1910, Walker decided to move again. Her new national headquarters would be in Indianapolis, Indiana. This midwestern city had a large and prosperous black business community. Walker met many new people there. One of them was a 24-year-old black attorney named Robert Lee Brokenburr. He had graduated from Howard University Law School.

Walker hired Brokenburr as the company's assistant manager. As her general manager, she hired another young attorney, Freeman Briley Ransom. The two men were loyal to Walker, and they worked well together. They were both part of a small but special group: young black American professionals. Walker knew they would take good care of her business while she traveled.

Everywhere she went, Walker signed up new agents and office workers. On a sales trip in Kentucky, she met a schoolteacher named Alice Kelly. Walker thought Kelly was unusually bright. She hired her and soon made her forewoman of the Indianapolis factory.

Walker liked and trusted Kelly. She even told her the company's hair-growing formula. It had been a secret known only by Walker and her daughter. Walker also hired one of Kelly's former students, Violet Davis Reynolds, as her private secretary.

Walker was pleased by her success, but she felt sad about one thing: she had never gone to school. She wanted to improve her skills. Here, Kelly proved useful. She gave Madam—all her employees called her that—advice on everything from which books to read to table manners to public speaking. Kelly often went along on Walker's business trips. She served her boss as both traveling companion and tutor.

Walker read several newspapers every morning. Whenever she saw a word she did not know, she asked Reynolds to look it up in the dictionary. She was trying to educate herself and her staff at the same time. Walker knew that her company needed intelligent workers.

C. J. Walker designed the company's advertisements. They showed Madam Walker before and after using Wonderful Hair Grower. The ads were very effective. By 1911, the Walker company had 950 agents and a monthly income of $1,000.

Walker found time for fun as well as for work. She liked to invite people to her house to listen to music or poetry. She bought a grand piano, a gold-covered harp, and a record player. Along with music, Walker loved the movies, which were then a brand-new kind of entertainment. A movie ticket cost 10 cents.

One afternoon, however, the movies made Walker unhappy. At the box office, she pushed a dime across to the ticket seller. The seller pushed it right back. She said the admission price for "colored persons" was now 25 cents. Walker was very angry—but she was not discouraged.

She went home and called an architect. She asked him to design a building big enough to hold her factory and her offices—and something else. When it was finished, the Walker Building covered a whole block in the middle of Indianapolis. It housed the factory, the offices—and the biggest and best movie house in Indianapolis. No black person would ever be treated rudely at this theater!

Many whites in Indianapolis were *prejudiced* against blacks. Walker's wealth and fame, however, meant she had less trouble than many others. Bankers, for example, treated her very politely. After all, she deposited thousands of dollars in her checking account each year.

Walker was also a good customer of the city's jewelry stores and automobile showrooms. They, too, gave her a warm reception. She loved cars and driving, and she became a very skillful driver. But she also had a chauffeur. On summer evenings, he would drive her around the city as she sat in the backseat of her big car.

In the midst of her success, Walker began to have serious disagreements with her husband. The

The Walker Building in Indianapolis, Indiana, housed a beauty shop and offices, as well as an elegant movie theater for the city's black residents.

couple finally agreed to end their marriage. Sarah Walker filed for divorce in late 1912, but she would retain her husband's name for the rest of her life. And for the rest of *his* life, C. J. Walker remained a Walker agent.

By the end of 1912, Walker had about 1,600 agents working for her. Now her company made almost $1,000 each *week*. She used most of the money to improve her business. She enlarged the factory, hired more people, and produced more products. Almost all her factory workers were black women who lived near the factory.

Meanwhile, A'Lelia had given her mother a wonderful gift. (For a short time, Lelia McWilliams was married to a man named Robinson. After she divorced him, she began calling herself A'Lelia Walker Robinson.) In 1912, A'Lelia adopted a daughter. This gave Madam Walker the title of grandmother, which pleased her very much.

A'Lelia's new daughter was 13-year-old Mae Bryant. Mae had long, beautiful hair, and she had served as a model for Walker products. After Mae joined the family, Walker started teaching her about the business. She often took her granddaughter on sales trips.

Mae heard her grandmother speak at many black business conventions. After almost every lecture, Walker's audience voted to name her the "foremost colored businesswoman in America." She was very proud of the title.

Walker's adopted granddaughter, Mae Bryant, had long, thick hair, which made her a good model for Walker products.

With Mae, Walker visited dozens of towns and cities. Mae helped her grandmother give her demonstrations and sign up new agents. She also gave out booklets about the Walker company. Mae and Walker usually traveled by train. Sometimes they passed by towns so small that they had no railroad stations. In these places, Mae tossed company booklets to the crowds waiting along the tracks.

In all the towns and cities they visited, Walker took orders. She sent them to Indianapolis. One day, Ransom wrote to Walker. "Your business is increasing here every day," he said. "I think you are the money making wonder of the age."

Ransom admired Walker, but he thought she sometimes spent too much money. She once sent him a letter saying that she had just spent $1,381.50 to buy her daughter a Cadillac. "I guess you think I am crazy," she wrote, "but I had a chance to get just what A'Lelia wanted in a car."

Ransom wrote back, "No, I don't think you crazy, but I think you very hard on your bank account." Then he added, "I take pleasure in the fact that there can hardly be anything else for you to buy, ha, ha!"

Meanwhile, A'Lelia Robinson was spending a lot of time in Harlem. This section of New York City was attracting black people from all over the country. Robinson believed that her mother should move there, and she started looking for a house.

Walker visited Harlem, and she loved it. The place was buzzing with politics, business, music, and theater. It gave her renewed energy. Wherever she went, the black community's most famous people surrounded her. They included composers, publishers, actors, poets, and businessmen.

In 1913, Robinson found a Harlem *town house* she liked. She talked her mother into buying it. Then she turned it into a combination home and beauty salon. When Walker saw it, she was delighted. "The Hair Parlor beats anything I have seen anywhere, even in the best Hair Parlors of the whites," she wrote Ransom. Others agreed. A local black newspaper called it "the most completely equipped and beautiful hair parlor that members of our Race ever had access to."

Walker agreed to move East. Before she went, she entertained a number of black leaders in Indianapolis. Some were journalists, some were politicians, and some were *civil rights* leaders. Walker listened to all of them, even if she did not agree with them. She sometimes argued with people who said Booker T. Washington was always right. Walker admired the great black spokesman, but she disagreed with him about women.

Washington did not think that women could be leaders. Walker, of course, knew they could. Still, she thought Washington was a brave man and a brilliant educator. She was always ready to praise any black person who wanted to help other blacks.

The night before she left Indianapolis, Walker gazed at a faded picture of her father. She was thinking about how far she had come in her 48 years. Only a short while earlier she had been struggling to support herself. Now she was helping to support orphanages and schools, and people called her Lady Bountiful. Only a short while earlier, few people had ever heard of her. Now she was called "the foremost businesswoman of the race."

An advertisement in a black-owned newspaper shows Walker's products and Walker herself. Her modeling of her own wares made them more attractive to African American women.

CHAPTER

5
Fighting
for Justice

Walker's elegant brick town house soon became a meeting place for Harlem's leaders. The four-story building also contained Lelia College and the Walker Hair Parlor. Walker's daughter and granddaughter helped her manage the college and the beauty parlor.

After Mae turned 19, however, the family had to get along without her. In 1916, Robinson enrolled her daughter in Spelman Seminary in

Atlanta, Georgia. This was the nation's first college for black women.

Meanwhile, the family business got better and better. Walker herself still worked as her company's chief sales agent. She seemed never to tire of giving speeches. A lecture she gave in Muskogee, Oklahoma, is typical of her style:

"I had little or no opportunity when I started out in life, having been left an orphan," she told a large audience of black women and men. "I had to make my own living and my own opportunity! But I made it! That is why I want to say to every Negro woman present, don't sit down and wait for the opportunities. . . . Get up and make them!"

Even if they never met her, the people who bought Walker's products felt close to her. This was at least partly because of her advertisements. Ads for other black cosmetics companies showed glamorous white women or light-skinned black women. Walker showed a black woman with black features—herself.

Walker was handsome but certainly not glamorous. Customers could say to themselves, "I could look like this." The advertisements seemed to say: Buy Walker's products and you will look like Walker! Look like Walker, and you will become successful, too!

A'Lelia Robinson (seated, front left) receives a Walker treatment in the Walker Hair Parlor in New York City while her adopted daughter, Mae Bryant (standing at left side of window), treats another customer.

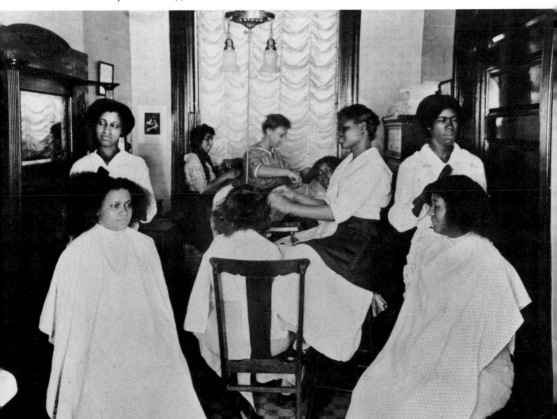

By 1926, there were 20,000 women and men selling Walker products. These agents often wrote to tell Walker how they felt about their jobs. One woman from Florida said happily, "I have all I can do at home and don't have to go out and work for white people in kitchens and factories."

A woman in Columbus, Ohio, wrote that she and her husband had bought a home and paid their debts. "Before I started out in Madam Walker's employ," she said, "I made the regular working woman's wage, but at this writing I average $23 a week." (At that time, female workers earned around $10 a week in the North and $2 a week in the South.)

Walker was sometimes called a "race woman." This term meant someone who was especially loyal to her or his own people. Walker not only hired mostly blacks; she also put her money back into the black community.

In 1916, for example, she built a *housing project* for black people in Indianapolis. To construct it, she employed 50 black construction workers. "My business is largely supported by my own people," she said. "So why shouldn't I spend my money so it will go back into colored homes? By giving my work to colored men . . . indirectly I am creating more jobs for our boys and girls."

Walker rarely rested. But by the fall of 1916, she was 48 years old. She decided she was ready to turn some of her road trips over to others. She would make one more trip, then quit traveling, she said.

This time, she visited cities in the South. She ended up in her Louisiana hometown. "Delta was honored Sunday," reported the local paper, "by a visit of the richest negro woman in the world, [Madam] C. J. Walker." In Delta, Walker walked down the muddy road to the cabin where she and her family had lived.

She stood outside, remembering her parents, remembering her childhood. No one, she said to herself, could have dreamed that little Sarah Breedlove would grow up to be rich and famous. She felt satisfied and proud.

In April 1917, soon after Walker returned to New York, the United States entered World War I. The war started black people talking all around the country. They asked each other an important question: should black men enlist to fight? Many said yes. They were sure that their country would respect their loyalty. But others believed differently. They thought that their country should grant them full rights as citizens before asking them to risk their lives.

This group had very real reason for concern. Violence against black people was bad and getting worse. The Ku Klux Klan wanted to keep blacks from being equal to whites. Klan "Knights" roamed the countryside, mostly in the South, burning fiery crosses. They beat, and even murdered, black people. Between 1885 and 1916, white mobs killed nearly 3,000 blacks.

But Walker and other well-known blacks believed that black Americans should "close ranks" with white Americans to help win the war.

They also believed that if blacks fought for their country, whites would treat them better.

Walker visited many army camps, where she encouraged young black recruits to become outstanding soldiers. After one such visit, she got a letter from a black sergeant. He said her words had "stayed with the boys longer than any spoken by anyone that I have known or heard of."

In the summer of 1917, bloody *race riots* swept several American cities. The worst of them took place in East St. Louis. In this Illinois city, mobs murdered 39 blacks, seriously injured hundreds of others, and drove thousands of black families from their homes.

After the East St. Louis riot, the nation's blacks felt both outrage and pain. Speaking for many of them, Walker said, "This is the greatest country under the sun. But we must not let our love of country cause us to abate one whit in our protest against wrong and injustice. We should protest until . . . such affairs as the East St. Louis riot be forever impossible."

Marchers stream down New York City's Fifth Avenue during the Negro Silent Protest Parade of 1917. A demonstration against antiblack violence, the parade was organized by Walker and her friends.

In July 1917, a committee of black leaders, including Walker, organized a *demonstration* against racial violence. It was called the Negro Silent Protest Parade. It took place in New York

City on July 28. About 10,000 black New Yorkers silently paraded down Fifth Avenue. The male marchers wore dark suits and carried banners and signs. One banner read: Treat Us so that We May Love Our Country. The female marchers, who included a number of Walker agents, wore white dresses. The women walked with rows of neatly dressed children. More than 20,000 people watched the Silent Parade. The watchers were also silent. The only sounds in the city seemed to come from the marchers' muffled drums and tramping feet.

The Negro Silent Protest Parade was orderly and peaceful. It was also very effective. It showed white America that black America was ready to stand up for its rights. The parade's success gave blacks a new feeling of strength. It promised hope for the future.

After helping to organize the Protest Parade, Walker kept on doing political work, and she was still very active in her business. Still, she found time to plan and build her dream house. In

Walker named her Irvington-on-Hudson, New York, mansion Villa Lewaro, derived from her daughter's name, Lelia Walker Robinson.

late 1916, she had bought a large piece of land in Irvington-on-Hudson, a town near New York City. All the people who lived there were white and rich.

At first, the people in Irvington did not like the idea of Walker's moving in. They asked why "a woman of her race" should live in their all-white town. But they changed their minds. Walker's new house was beautiful—it had 30 rooms, huge gardens, and a swimming pool—and Walker soon proved herself a quiet, pleasant resident. "Instead of dislike, her neighbors have learned to respect her," said one citizen of the town.

One of Walker's first guests in her new home was Ida B. Wells-Barnett. Wells-Barnett was a newspaperwoman and a worker for black civil rights. She had first met Walker several years earlier. Wells-Barnett said Walker's success "made me take pride anew in Negro womanhood."

Several weeks after Wells-Barnett's visit, Walker's *blood pressure* shot up. Now her doctors told her something she did not want to hear. They said if she wanted to stay alive, she "must give little or no attention again to business or heavy social activities."

In this portrait, Walker shows all the grace and confidence that she had once envied in other women.

CHAPTER

6
The Legacy

World War I ended in November 1918. Walker
helped greet the returning black *veterans*, then
went back to work. By the following January, her
company had become black America's most successful business. Sales for 1918 had topped a
quarter of a million dollars. Sales for 1919 promised to be even higher.

Walker's company was healthy, but she was
not. In early 1919, her doctor, Colonel Joseph
Ward, put his foot down: Walker's blood pressure
was soaring, he said. She must leave her company

in the hands of her very capable employees. Walker obeyed Ward's orders—more or less. She spent fewer hours in the office and on road trips, but more time on political activity.

Walker felt very strongly about what America owed its black war veterans. "Their country called them to defend its honor on the battlefield of Europe," she said, "and they have bravely, fearlessly bled and died that that honor might be maintained."

These men, she pointed out, "will soon be returning. To what? . . . To being strung up, riddled with bullets, burned at the stake? No! A thousand times no! . . . They will come back to face like men whatever is in store for them and like men defend themselves, their families, and their homes."

Walker also said that she did not want "to encourage in any way a conflict between the two races." She advised the returning soldiers to live quiet, peaceful lives. But, she added, if "prejudiced" persons "infringe upon their rights as men," the veterans should "resent the insult like men."

In April 1919, Dr. Ward's fears came true. Walker became seriously ill. As a nurse and doctor stood by her bedside, she talked about all her unfinished business. She intended to build a girls' school in Africa. She planned to construct a new office building and factory. She also wanted to put up a housing development for the poor in Indianapolis.

Her first move was to donate $5,000 to the *National Association for the Advancement of Colored People's (NAACP)* fund for *antilynching*. The gift was announced at an NAACP conference in New York. The 2,500 people at the conference stood up and cheered. Walker's contribution was the largest the organization had ever received.

Walker received hundreds of get-well messages. "God spare you to the race and humanity," said one of them. But Dr. Ward was not hopeful about his patient. He said her high blood pressure had hopelessly damaged her kidneys. After she heard this, Walker started making more gifts.

"Madam Walker gave $25,000 to colored organizations and institutions," reported the *New York Age* newspaper. "Intimate friends believe she fully realizes the seriousness of her condition and wanted to do what she could for deserving race institutions before passing away."

A few days later, Walker's nurse heard her say, "I want to live to help my race." Then she slipped into a coma, or state of unconsciousness. On the following Sunday morning, the Chicago *Defender* later reported, the day "dawned bright and warm. Outside, where the trees and lawn were green and pretty, the flowers blooming and the birds merrily singing, all was gaiety and happiness.

"Inside, where several people gathered around a beautiful four-posted bed and watched a magnificent soul go into eternity, all was grief and sorrow." Then Ward "turned to those around the bedside and said, 'It is over.'" Sarah Breedlove Walker, 51 years old, died on May 25, 1919.

One thousand people came to Walker's funeral. The service ended with a reading of her favorite Bible passage, Psalm 23. "Farewell, farewell, a long farewell," said the minister. Then A'Lelia, Mae, and a circle of weeping friends took Walker's rose-covered casket to Woodlawn cemetery.

Tributes began to pour in at once. One of Walker's friends, pioneering educator Mary McLeod Bethune, said Walker's life was "the clearest demonstration, I know, of Negro woman's ability recorded in history. She has gone, but her work still lives and shall live as an inspiration to not only her race but to the world."

Journalist and author George Samuel Schuyler wrote, "What a boon it was for one of their own race to stand upon the pinnacle and exhort the womanhood of her race to come forth [and] lift up their heads." W. E. B. Du Bois said, "It is given to few persons to transform a people in a generation. Yet this was done by the late Madam C. J. Walker. . . . [She] made and deserved a fortune and gave much of it away generously."

Walker's concern for needy people became even clearer after her death. Her will listed dozens of organizations and individuals. She established a $100,000 trust fund for "worthy charities." She also left sums ranging from $2,000 to $5,000 to many different groups. These included the Colored Orphans' Home in St. Louis, the Home for Aged and Infirm Colored People in Pittsburgh, the Haines Institute in Georgia, the NAACP, and Tuskegee Institute.

Walker was America's first black self-made female millionaire. But she never forgot her roots. She was born poor, but she eagerly shared her immense wealth with the needy. She had no early education, but she made a point of supporting schools. Her parents were former slaves, but she stood up for her rights as an American citizen.

She used her fortune and personal power to help her community, and she urged others to follow her lead.

Walker's success came from more than cosmetics. She taught black women to develop their natural beauty. This improved their sense of worth and made them more self-confident. The Walker company employed thousands of people. Today, countless black Americans can name a relative—an aunt, a grandmother, perhaps an uncle—who served as a Walker agent. Walker's products helped these women and men to educate their children, build homes, and start their own businesses.

Walker often talked about her life. She told the story to encourage other black people to pursue their dreams. "I promoted myself," she said. "I had to make my own living and my own opportunity! But I made it! Don't sit down and wait for the opportunities to come. Get up and make them!"

Walker relaxes at Villa Lewaro. Despite the calm she displays in this picture, Walker was a very busy woman, traveling all over the country to promote her products and leading an active political and social life.

70

Walker had great courage and imagination. Those qualities carried her from a cotton field to a mansion. They took her from being unknown and poor to being famous and wealthy. Her example continues to inspire Americans who want to improve their own lives and to help others as well.

Further Reading

Other Biographies of Madam C. J. Walker

Bundles, A'Lelia Perry. *Madam C. J. Walker: Entrepreneur.* New York: Chelsea House, 1991.

Related Books

Greenfield, Eloise. *Mary McLeod Bethune.* New York: Crowell, 1977.

Jacobs, William Jay. *Great Lives: Human Rights.* New York: Scribner, 1990.

McKissack, Patricia, and Fredrick McKissack. *The Story of Booker T. Washington.* Chicago: Childrens Press, 1991.

Meltzer, Milton, ed. *The Black Americans: A History in Their Own Words.* New York: Crowell, 1984.

Myers, Walter Dean. *Now Is Your Time: The African-American Struggle for Freedom.* New York: HarperCollins, 1991.

Sterne, Emma Gelders. *Mary McLeod Bethune.* New York: Knopf, 1957.

Young, Bernice Elizabeth. *Harlem: The Story of a Changing Community.* New York: Messner, 1972.

Glossary

antilynching   opposed to the practice of putting someone to death, especially by hanging, through mob action without legal approval

blood pressure   the amount of pressure put on the walls of blood vessels by the blood they contain; if a person's blood pressure is too high, it can damage the vessels

bollworm   a type of caterpillar that feeds on unripe cotton

civil rights   the personal and property rights of an individual recognized by a government and its laws and constitution

demonstration   a public display of group feelings toward a person or cause

housing project   a group of similar houses or apartments built for low-income families

literacy   the ability to read and write

National Association for the Advancement of Colored People (NAACP)   organization founded in 1909 that challenged segregation and discrimination

74

nutrition   the taking in of food that promotes growth and health

prejudice   a feeling or opinion, usually negative, that has been formed about something or someone before all the facts are known

race riots   mob action, usually violent, that is motivated by fear of or anger toward people of another race

racist   marked by the belief that one's own race is superior

sharecropper   a tenant farmer who is given supplies, works the land, and receives an agreed-upon portion of the crop, minus charges

slave   a person who is owned as property by another

town house   a single-family house of two or three stories that is connected to a similar house by a common sidewall

veteran   a former member of the armed services

yellow fever   an acute, destructive, infectious disease marked by fever and jaundice and caused by a virus carried by the mosquito

Chronology

1867 Sarah Breedlove is born on December 23 in Delta, Louisiana.

1874 Sarah's parents die in a yellow fever epidemic.

1878 Sarah moves to Vicksburg, Mississippi, with her sister, Louvenia.

1882 Sarah marries Moses McWilliams.

1885 Her daughter, Lelia, is born.

1887 Moses McWilliams dies; Sarah and her daughter move to St. Louis, Missouri.

1905 Sarah moves to Denver, Colorado, and develops the formula for Wonderful Hair Grower.

1906 She marries Charles Joseph Walker and changes her name to Madam C. J. Walker.

1908 Madam C. J. Walker moves to Pittsburgh and opens Lelia College.

1910   Walker moves to Indianapolis and has a factory built for the manufacture of her hair-care products.

1912   Walker travels throughout the United States selling her products and speaking to major black organizations; she donates $1,000 to a black YMCA in Indianapolis; she divorces C. J. Walker; Walker becomes a grandmother when her daughter adopts Mae Bryant.

1916   Walker moves to Harlem in New York City.

1917   She helps to organize the Negro Silent Protest Parade in New York City.

1918   Walker moves into Villa Lewaro, a Hudson River mansion; she becomes a millionaire; Walker is diagnosed with high blood pressure and is told to strictly limit her activities.

1919   Walker contributes large sums of money to the NAACP antilynching fund and other causes; she dies on May 25 at Villa Lewaro.

Index

Marian W. Taylor, former editor of the *New York Times* and *Los Angeles Times* syndicates, also served as an editor at *Life* magazine. Currently a New York City–based book editor and writer, she is coauthor of the *Facts on File Dictionary of New Words* and author of *Harriet Tubman* in the Chelsea House BLACK AMERICANS OF ACHIEVEMENT series and *Chief Joseph* in the Chelsea House NORTH AMERICAN INDIANS OF ACHIEVEMENT series.

Picture Credits